Surprise Visit

Thomas Fink

the Domestic press

© 1993 The Domestic Press
All rights reserved
323 E. 8th Street
New York, NY 10009

ISBN 0-934450-54-4
first published 1993
2 4 6 8 10 9 7 5 3

Distributed with
the help of
Unmuzzled Ox
105 Hudson Street
New York, NY 10013

Cover Design by Doug Levere

Grateful acknowledgement
is made to the
following publications
where poems appeared:

New Observations: "Elite Sands"
Zone 3: "Sermon" (in "The Ethel Landsman Poems")

for Joseph and Beatrice Fink

Contents

I.

Xanthippe's Diary	1
The Ethel Landsman Poems	4
Twinges	6
Wallace Stevens	8
Willem de Kooning	9
Minimalist	12
Andy	13
Louise Bourgeois	14
For My Daughter	15

II.

Prolegomenon to a Respectful Distance	17
Wonder Their Chance	18
Unemployed Sibyl	19
Between Molecules	20
Status	21
Cholesterol Elixir	22
Cathartic Choices	23
Fortune Cookies	24

III.

Cult	29
For the Claimants	30
Sunset	31
Target	32
Gold Flaw	33
Press Release	34
Glass Zone	35
Winter Elegy	36
Gas Legacy	37

IV.

Deficit Ramp	41
Poison Justice	43
Confirmation Hearings	44
Bandaid	45
Collapsible	46
The Rub	47
Elite Sands	48
Skipping LP	50
Note	55

I.

Xanthippe's Diary

1

lost keys—
your sun rises underground

don't step down

2

the boys purchase doubt
cheap market—
shoes that
hate feet

3

wind husband translated
driftwood sentences cave hones—
count stains on sand

4

the good the good good prattle breakfast—
to whom for whom
good?

noble
sh(r)ed livelihood
weighty entertainer

I gender captive scrub—
our three shoots
abstracted to bodysoul
hunger

you a much (p)raised
vanishpoint

5

heap continually
grime stench tunics—
to wash
philosophy's exertions

four decades scorn
and no
crumb footnote—
what whose purity
borrowed earned (un)attained?

6

more time so glibly
discardable?
pierless soul

endowed circus
adolescent mandolins — you
drank loftily
conclusion

they yanked me home—
my sober
common truth syringe
disabled

7

shrew me histories—
fuck the boys can't
know me

don't midwives
respect blood
question flow blood—
unteachable seducer cringed
behind script

8

they fetish slobber
his leftovers—
would instant burn this—
take hide my daughter

lost keys—
your sun rises underground

don't step down

The Ethel Landsman Poems

1. Mutability Canto

Some old people,
they make themselves blonde.
How does blonde come to a wrinkled face?

Yes, yes, time runs out at you.
I used to have such a good vision—
even the smallest print I could read—
and beautiful wavy hair.
Now, like anything else,
no eyes, no teeth, no hair.
Nothing means to me anything.

Oh well, to bear and grin it:
I love the air because I'm used to it.

2. Even the elevators

The other schul–
it wasn't like this so religious.
Even the elevators.

You can't touch Saturday the elevators.

It takes you up;
you don't touch it.
I went up;
I was myself.
The man told me.

3. Sermon

Do you want some juice a drink?
Come, I have.
And papaya dried.
No sugar:
God put in the sugar.
I always said, fruit and vegetables.
I think I was the first one.

Close your chest.
Do you believe in being warm dressed to
  your body?
Later, it will get you arthritis, the cold.
Could be chronicle.

You're always with writing and with
  reading,
reading and writing.
You took up a professional that kills the
  eyes.

I used to do everything the teeth of my
  skin.
But if you're careful is nothing dangerous.

Eventually, once you'll click it;
just don't despair.
Everything good'll come in your way.

Twinges

stiffly throat
relearning iron—
appease
ancestral gate

never to rebuff
ponderous history—
cling burden
comb elaborate breath

homework clogs—
late feet—
behind sister's cantata

foregoing gland
gown blushes want—
helpless floor

button powder
wilt secret—
and not much anything

trim praise
brushed back—
borrowed pen matters
refine cracks

pink year?
unworried sk(e)in—
douse noon
awake

too masterful
napkin

if house sudden
lenience
compose a gusto—
reasonable climax assured

Wallace Stevens

In his memos
the suited giant
assumes winter.

First words,
first winds
renew one to hungers.

These are to be amended
variously to prepare
for the strain toward

proper impossibles,
precise thuds.
He beckons us

to concoct insurance
that can honestly be sold.

Willem De Kooning

1

whose arms legs putty
extend, surge, flail
thousand limbs extending one raw field—
attic stuff only sometimes and briefly
extricable by an eye unused to such
incalculable densities

agitate mass theatre—
from thirty heights rain falls
to stop midair(s)—
and behind all this is it mystified
to infer some potent
unconscious some rare secret
trapped
or some being (left on the other side
of the Atlantic) crazily blanketed with lyric
   storm
breathing asthma?
if mere supportive air
one works hard for it

2

"remember not a woman
not paradigm for woman after a history of
   framed
inadequacies
but a collapse

knifing the impertinence of simulacrum"

yet farce loop breasts
brutal bracelet teeth and teeth again the
  neckline
straddling bicycle—
paint fleshes ever in all directions—
what's then the monster?
a certain seeing's pummeled those
  obliged to pose—
such ardent fascist repetition—
that more than corset stress—
but thousand thousand caresses and
slashes defocusing
do they ever release her
from one perfect embalming?

3

explode masses euphemized landscape—
newspaper treading water—dunes whisper
  your mark
random nature
as those mindless

if woman man returns water
rips the stitches no intestines please I cannot
stomach— or waters
come at once all colors
you would never huddle—
impasto's hardened you think
of drowning pleasure this is not water

4

long past the reckless
thirst cedar bravura
is the ancient coming home to calm
primaries?

white scape breathing evenly
blue silk stabilities
edging to violet
benevolent yellow
a vibrant blood
pouring pliant limbs

who has freed murk captives?
observers tell us no mind—
perfected
unaffected eye hand only—
his own ruminations
left somewhere
unclaimed

Minimalist

handwriting like blush odor
you demand stringent marble

think edge—
square enough empire—
platform atom limn

again tenant shirks
contract—
guess edit perennial—
unsnared equation predicament

swarm interstices

Andy

visceral keyhole
liberating calamity
missile frolic

flounce camp
hegemony—
boycott truth

bubble you nourish soup—
chuckle erase need

Lousie Bourgeois

I fear therefore—
stone

family sleeping white—
white famine

Mother Reason
track your man

inside the cube
I am my own

eyes years
drill questions in the proud cube—
drill to restore

For My Daughter

intimacy chooses—
blood moon
water moon—
delicate night poured

grows you

plenty mouth—
windy howl
storming this sleep
spreading name

II.

Prolegomenon to a Respectful Distance

Since you live
another mind,
I wrote you.
To extend mine?

At midnight, alone, cop(y)ing,
you assume access
to my terrain,
but there's only—

blind witness,
tonguetied intercom.

Wonder Their Chances

across bonds that wound
physically
unhatched makes
boundaries wonder their chances

f(r)iction a steel paper
ceiling
pulse the irate
distortions

edge thinking lapse
stance—
hopefully from
the is to the a

Unemployed Sibyl

and why wouldn't I miss my
delectable sinecure?

being used to work
doxically—
some clear (if by your fashionable
standards simplistic)
reverence for the whole
presiding

even over the most
inclement classics
and every hubbub ultimately
dissolving
to affirm tenets

Between Molecules

between molecules
    moles

a dozen minds
thinning
    in booths
    chill berths
    snail boats

who dozing resolutely
give birth
to no king

no
body I

Status

If something
as fate
may eat one's
assiduously earned
oats,
credits,
et cetera,

why then
does the luck-
baiting brat
insist on prattling
about his slick new
untested
boat?

Day eats
the date; some
choke.

Cholesterol Elixir

after marble breath
flames sweetly

relief

ant-print
one finally detects—
many insinuated
althoughs

can I risk repeatedly this
thickening future?
can I
afford today
symptom utter blade?

Cathartic Choices

Enduring
closet guilt?
Quilt it,
and burn quietly.

Singled out
(somewhat
deservedly perhaps)
for public guilt?
Quilt quickly a
repertoire of quips
and display
most publicly;

if reviled further,
burn it loudly,
as cameras pan.

Should condition persist,
just quit.

Fortune Cookies

1

you never bleed
unless
there's a pivotal
point to be made

and never so
copiously
as to stain

clarity

2

if introspection's
capable of interface
you may soon find your home
computer
problem-crunching
has rendered unfeasible
human intimacies

if so I implore:
neither lambaste
inanimate hardware
       (for one makes countless choices
       from a vast menu)
nor burrow in subroutines
for cost-
benefit ratio

3

masturbate promiscuously
avoid expressways

eschew transfusions
and date chastely

some lethal ills
will sail elsewhere

4

I could tell you in a booming voice

that you have the capacity
to slaughter thousands

or the capacity to enable thousands
to burst out of miserable confinement

such unearned influence is too tempting—
how can I calculate?

"your smile puts people at ease
but be sure to keep tabs on hidden
  anger"—

unlikely to boomerang

5

down to the particle
thick and thin paperbacks
have administered your
joyless diets

or systematically
commanded you not to diet
    yet promised obliquely
        the loss that has always eluded

shed them

in time
you will be thin
as you were mea(n)t
to be

6

you are a normal joe
when you have to be
to break even
    but unlike many in your practical
        shoes
    you do not fetichize normality

the basement serves—
    I won't
    tell the rest of 'em—
diverse blisses

7

soon after the current recession
goes underground
fruits of a thousand-to-one gamble
will let you
pay off that acre of debts
        but whether you'll wake up to
   how damned lucky
        you'll have been
        and may never again—

stop me if I'm boring you

8

anonymous I
anonymous you—

my careful words
walk
innumerable tightropes

9

we've all
had it with yòur shabby-
ego-bit—
many dead people
have loved you

10

you once believed that a rare ambiance
was awaiting your arrival
but now you can stay put

III.

Cult

to breathe ABANDON
LEASE true home
to love sublimely SEVER
BAND dearest one
to pluck DRIVE
BANDWAGON your singular
lute to beckon LEAK
SILVER jackpot at
last become RECANT
BONE substantial

until rash vapor lease
ragged bone
luteless home

For the Claimants

deeming themselves
foregone
to shirk loyal blood

the claimants axe the looming effigies
castrate phantoms
plant mystical the ancestors

to club exile

but as their own productions
answer eerily in thronged voices
they will learn

in this pit they have buried
prior seeds—
whose logic creeping back
from umbilical underground

rises to embrace them

Sunset

anomalous need's
passion yawn

cope harlequin quixotic trellis
throb parlor
to ice desires

clenched wi(n)dow
shriek knob
apt blue leap

Target

blood stance
cool river acolyte—
stripped magenta humble smooth

weightless discipline

almost binge—
slake stride—
submit
vine sprouting ridge
slide chrome sprawl tendon

clean gawk leaping name—
stoop flood—
slantwise taboo
must not trample—
oil smuggled kiss stood

Gold Flaw

quake avarice
beef custard water—
melt v(o)ices tre(m)ble
slam

to prove undersoil
sprawl fountains— fasten
gold flaw—
pork blush
flurry dignity blunt flesh monk

dispersal autumn
effortless snow

yet unsurmounted
hammock ethos—
inch message wise to sleeve

Press Release

cordons of sex police rented background
  dawn
entice weekends sobbing fist code
victor you loser her real name is no
bonfire gossip corrupting obscene telex
  skyward

bypass naked jeep bed ballroom
flowing legs barricade hoax
will makes wall oh say can you mess an
  inch
intently beheaded ultimately they must
speedboat inches whip orgies

groove booze stigma brace amiably
blameless stronghold booth ploughing
  saga
boos spineless raid molehill envy
stupid bastion dope shame listlessly
steam bash howl the carpet

bail skullcap glamor riff the grass

Glass Zone

death sugar the boiled
lips renouncing teeth

cut shadow
through needle door
aghast lawn closing heights

dim throat
pleas for psalm juice
twig uphold
darling darling umbrella
or wax

Winter Elegy

radical stock crystal summons—
grassroots elite underdog
to faithful wheel—
headfirst et cetera you fodder go along

parched rhythm dapper frazzling—
tedious erase flesh

nervous doubt plaza relentless—
pit screams

they harvest martyr—
obit ink violin futureless wince

winter our dead—-
weeping bones forgiveness quivers—
penetrates grass

Gas Legacy

drooling for original sunlight
elusive apex—
your breath dedicated to lightning
blood credo signed

someone nabbed you
across fetish—
sumptuous mist slumber rush

yours is agile
blowhards gas legacy—
you ash doubt

tag along with retro futurists
prop pinnacle leftovers—
sham(ble)s ostensible gold

resolute sycophant
humble braggart—
whose palacè?

not all of us make
gullible doors

omitted bulb reproach
scrape alibi—
rearview
these caption histrionics
fuzz out

clockwork passion
you lob(by) joy—
urgent chestnut bullet
eat soundbite

waddle placard
stooge—
agelong lemon dream—
sparse icarus sunning wax

bequeathed ruin? outside
refuge

IV.

Deficit Ramp

flaws signed
slyly or unseen—
no shame repair
hurried stitches
(though intricate parts allegedly
flown in from afar)
sedating
recession autos

norm to
work awkwardness

shuttle ills
collective bubble sustained
another quarter—
many of those fallen
brush off to borrow no questions

no willingness
to pause—
blip doubt

take deficit ramp—
all other
lanes shut
indefinitely

nestegg rampage—
almost mattress mentality—
mundane bottom lifestyling

as virus mavens
access none of their business—
another abstract medicine
to sell furiously

slam tanker oil's sudden
incontinence—
tomorrow's sharper bite

new bulbs
that won't write—
legalese warranties who has
resources to spend a year in small
claims?

sponsor cheerful shortcut—
additional plastic (no I will not mirror
the nations this way)

most cog whippersnappers as
per usual—
promo irate reckless
disservices—
the customer always
a non so chill dude your
bloodpressure

Poison Justice

prophet bubbles
confess your robes

thunder banners proof—
violent wine

cold title a wry sieve

dictate hiss knell—
remilk the knife

drink always another ghost—
unvanquished echo

no repeal—
parted lids pay calendar

Confirmation Hearings

gown rectitude
fondle that protocol
prettify anathema

jaw dance
dupe
mountaintop
squirt marble
fiasco

gender farming
torrid bandit faith

I warden bottle
static the singsong
genuflect zeal defective

ruthless placards
uppity corn hole
have
emaciated

Bandaid

servile bigot's
nutshell study:
"address the bane wedlock:
mutual domicile
failing annulment"

our anxious hegemony puts out
churlish almsgiving
(no parity)
blooping fulsome an
occasional
pseudo amity

to plug minimum pink honor

Collapsible

athwart cancer
floodgate industries
leak thunderstorm
kiss loudly nuclear
skeleton flames

insuperable cordless arteries
soundproof id(ea)
narrow stars
greenhouse wrinkles
deafening womb

o rational miser
loophole kingpin
eyestrain futurist
enough you

The Rub

Robed officiously
in shrubs, a
self-anointed
microbic sovereign

enlists all manner of
rubbish to rein in
short-term profitability.
With pernicious micro-

structured precision,
it robs
very rain of
precious ointment.

Elite Sands

fireball a thousand peaces

rockeye trolling—
boomer choreography

minimal pain prevail
and quick quick

blitz elite sands—
acrid looting hole ablaze

slit meekly its cities

tornado shield—
vulture rain pillage awash—
chemical light fills the breasts

who (s)oil aqua blame?

foiled skirmish warehouse—
smoke rot backpedalling

guesswork aircraft—
payload air supreme

sadbushwar
deluding embargo—
stammering counter madman—
jubilant rumble whisper death

collateral horror—
not uncommon fire friend

husband your outcome—
next day bang

precisionguided gunspeak—
no contamination—
electronic debris— legit
bombast fell back to earth

dogfight leaflets—
near starvation base

deprive winter—
would I weep?

won't be home if we don't bomb it

supply route craters—
expel the century

what's to mediate?
patch up limbs—
harass again the air

children who will not wave

Skipping LP

for Stephen Paul Miller

the real question is weather—
rural real reel
America
    does the man bleed?
    video proof blanked insanely
so glad I took schedule
out of my time
to meet you fine
    city no mightstick's colorblind—
    shambles (y)our neighborhood
    example (and more
    later)
and that democrat hill club
lynching
almost my
bootstrap Supreme
    you need high
    ceilings not cavelettes
    for more than token bootstrapping
blessed wonderful with real
parents and a very wonderful....
    did you really clean up
    your mess over there?
    oil sticks to everything
shuddup and lemme sprocket:
I commander-in-cheer
in-cheese—

having presided over the supreme kicking
  of ass
        alleged vanquished
        still acting
        victorious a year later
since the last untelevised war—-
support our tropes
        default loan deficit joblessness
        (abundant famine)
        and who
        underwrites an additional
bottom line
that that that darn bully
hasn't complied—
the United
Nations does not play
mindgames
        whopper yankee-feel-good
        slugfest?
                brand taxpayer cattle
                eventually no alternative
that liberal liberal liberal
libel Congress— now
there I've
said it
        deregulation (i.e. Reagan)
        revolution dwindling
        separation of greenchurch and
           state
go forward to
tomorrow past:
to the back to the back
        never factored headlong
        doddering of central
        gears producing massive
        collapse rushing workers to unmarked

        retirement
crisis anybody turns
family
family my family
I am
and proud
        paper vigor paper growth
        champagne 80's
        flattened—
        crystal ball:
        Porkrind Kingpin slated as
        delayed victim
and respect gentlemen
for things I didn't do—
how then could I know
that I would be
this room today?
I didn't live
this century
        would tattoo prohibitions
        but ambivalent Supreme
        gestures—
        does the man
        bleed?
I'm very fortunate—
I have
        electric breadwinners
        microchip labor—
        holistic designer crime
         farms
        no match for rising sum
        and common markup
right across the eyes
I am the future you make—
it's where
I came from

        illiterate ears
        contagious history?
And ours working well
to make the mike work a very important
        never bigscreen thespian?
        don't be cocksure
        about owning
        means of seduction
mike works
            "appearance is
            reality"
            opines the shirt
believe family—
have our platform
        world family planet dwellers
        air water soil—
        finally
        undo murder before millenium
        and keep on next thousand years
a very good family have a very good
  family—
to be a we
in—
one of the things is to talk about it

Note

p. 6-7 The Ethel Landsman Poems:

Ethel Landsman (1888-1986)
left her native Odessa, Russia in 1905
and settled in New York City.
Between 1977 and 1986, I collected
numerous phrases and sentences
spoken by her. A number of these
appear in the poems.

A "schul" is Yiddish for synagogue, and
"ruggeleh" is a kind of pastry.

Thomas Fink,
born in New York, N.Y. in 1954,

received a B.A. from Princeton University and a Ph.D. from Columbia University in English. He is an associate professor of English at LaGuardia Community College, City University of New York.

His book, **The Poetry of David Shapiro**, is published by Farleigh Dickinson University Press (of Associated University Presses).

His poems have appeared in *Zone 3, Manhattan Poetry Review, Bad Henry Review, Community Review, New Observations,* and elsewhere.

His literary criticism has been published in *American Poetry Review, Twentieth Century Literature, Minnesota Review, Modern Poetry Studies, Nouvelle Europe, American Letters and Commentary,* and several other journals.

His paintings are in several private collections.